# 5 MINUTE HISTORY

SCOTT ADDINGTON

# FIRST WORLD WAR
# WEAPONS

First published 2014

The History Press
The Mill, Brimscombe Port
Stroud, Gloucestershire, GL5 2QG
www.thehistorypress.co.uk

British Library Cataloguing in Publication Data.
A catalogue record for this book is available from the British Library.

ISBN 978 0 7524 9322 0

Typesetting and origination by The History Press
Printed in Europe

# CONTENTS

# INTRODUCTION

THE FIRST WORLD War was the first conflict that had a truly global reach. It was also one of the most deadly, with 35 million casualties, of which 14 million were killed. It was a brutal war of attrition with thousands of soldiers killed and seriously wounded every day; indeed, the true casualty numbers are very difficult, if not impossible, to comprehend for those of us who were not actually there to witness the carnage.

It was also a war of technology and of invention. The science of killing advanced so rapidly during the four years of the conflict that the weapons and tactics employed by the relevant armies, navies and air forces of 1918 were unrecognisable from those in use when war broke out in the late summer months of 1914.

Many technologies that are now the staple of modern warfare can trace their origins to the First World War, such as the tank, the fighter plane and anti-aircraft guns. More traditional weapons, such as the machine gun, grenades and artillery, also enjoyed significant tactical and technological advancement during the war, allowing them to become even more effective killing machines than they were before.

In putting this 5 Minute History together it has been impossible to include every weapon that was used during the war. Instead I have included those that had the greatest impact on the soldiers who lived, fought and died in the trenches, on the water or above the lines in the skies of Europe.

I hope you enjoy the brief overviews of some of the main weapons and technologies that were used during the war, and are inspired to go out and read some of the more in-depth analysis of these weapons that can be found in bookshops or online.

*SMA*
*Spring 2014*

# ARTILLERY

WITHOUT DOUBT, ARTILLERY was the king of the battlefield. Despite the devastating firepower of the machine gun, the threat of the tank and the daring and dash of the fighter pilots high above the trenches, it was to the artillery gun that all the combatant armies turned to when they were in search of a breakthrough.

The artillery in use during the First World War could be split into two distinct groups: field artillery and heavy artillery. Field artillery at that time consisted of light, horse-drawn guns that were relatively quick to set up and break down, enabling them to keep pace with infantry and cavalry. The heavier guns were much bigger and less easy to move around; they were transported on wheeled carriages, transported in pieces to the front and assembled in situ, or carried on the back of modified railway carriages.

At the beginning of the war, field artillery was the order of the day. Most armies had decent numbers of field guns, as they were ideally suited to the mobile wars of the nineteenth century. There were two main types of field artillery. The first fired a high-velocity round using a relatively flat trajectory, often against targets that were in the open and within sight of the guns. The second type was the howitzer, which fired a slower round at a higher trajectory. These were more effective against an enemy that was taking cover behind buildings or earthworks. Field artillery was able to fire relatively rapidly. The famous French *soixante-quinze* (seventy-five) gun boasted a revolutionary recoil system in which only the barrel moved and not the whole gun; this allowed up to twenty-five rounds per minute to be fired by a well-drilled crew. In comparison, the crew of a similar-sized British gun would only be able to muster around eight rounds per minute.

The light field guns dominated proceedings in the early months of the war, but as the trench system began to take shape towards the end of 1914 and the mobile war disappeared, at least on the Western Front, all of the belligerents began to appreciate the immediate need for much heavier guns that were able to smash enemy defences, disperse barbed wire and destroy dugouts and strongpoints. It wasn't long before factories all over Europe were churning out vast quantities of heavy guns and equally heavy ammunition.

As in other areas of First World War weaponry, Germany initially had the upper hand in terms of numbers and technological advancement when it came to big artillery guns. In August 1914 a handful of Krupp-made 42cm guns (nicknamed 'Big Berthas') and a dozen or so Skoda 12in howitzers reduced the

## I WAS THERE

You had to thrust the shell into the breech, ram it home, and then push in the charge that would fire it, which was explosive held in a canvas bag shaped something like a mushroom with two smaller charges in canvas bags behind it. They were called 'cores' and it was physical hard work. The gun-drill was just as it had been in the old days and the weapon was really obsolete. Once you'd loaded the gun it was fired by pulling a lanyard and, of course, the guns themselves took a fair bit of man-handling.

Gunner N. Tennant, 11th Howitzer Battery, Royal Artillery[1]

supposedly impregnable fortress complex of Liège to rubble in a matter of days, much to the shock of the Allies. The Allied manufacturing machine quickly got up to speed, however, and achieved some level of parity.

With the design of artillery there was always a trade off – the bigger and heavier the shell became, the shorter the distance it could be fired over. As the war progressed, the general trend on all sides was to make heavier shells to cause maximum damage. In 1914 the shell of a standard German howitzer was 15lb. In 1916 that had grown to 28lb, with a range of 23,500yd, and then a year later the 21cm-'long mortar' boasted a shell of 261lb but with a range of only 11,200yd. The biggest guns on show during the war were those mounted on railway carriages. Some had a specialist mount that allowed the gun to be pivoted to provide a large field of fire. Others had a fixed direction of fire, but the wagons they were mounted on could be moved along

### DID YOU KNOW?

German manufacturer Krupp made the biggest gun of the war. Nicknamed the 'Paris Gun', it was capable of firing a 260lb shell over 80 miles. From March to August 1918 it fired over 300 shells at Paris.

a curved piece of track. These guns, although they had potentially massive destructive power, were easily spotted by enemy air observation crews and as a consequence had to be constantly on the move, which limited their effectiveness.

As the general shift towards bigger guns continued, transporting them into place became a serious issue, especially in remote regions. In 1914 the standard means of moving artillery pieces around were wheeled wagons pulled by horses or mules. By 1918 the horse and wagon was still the primary mode of transport, despite the huge weight of the guns. Many of the roads up to the front were under constant enemy fire and often smashed to pieces, while the rest of the landscape was often a churned up muddy bog; as a result, mechanised transportation was limited in where it could be effectively used.

The manning of the guns varied according to the size and type of gun, but for a typical field artillery piece a team of six was common: a non-commissioned officer in command who received and gave out orders, a layer who was responsible for the gun's alignment and elevation, a gunner responsible for opening and closing the breech, and three men for handling shells and fuses.

Apart from for the very long-range guns, artillery targeting was directed by watching where the shells landed. This role was mostly carried out by a forward observation officer, who occupied a post near to the front and relayed messages back to the gun by flags or telephone. This role was also taken on by aerial artillery spotters in balloons, kites or planes. For the very big guns, aerial spotting was the only way to confirm accuracy of fire. Pilots would drop notes of where the shells landed for the gunners.

# RIFLES AND BAYONETS

THROUGHOUT THE WAR, rifles formed the bedrock of infantry weapons. The machine gun may have offered an unprecedented rate of fire, but it was cumbersome and the crews on both sides found it difficult to haul it over no-man's-land during advances. Machine-gun crews also tended to be targeted, once located, by enemy artillery and concentrated small-arms fire. Trench mortars were often scarce and grenades were cumbersome to carry in large numbers in the heat of battle. The rifle, however, along with its bayonet, was a constant companion to infantrymen on all sides.

By 1914, all the major belligerents had been independently manufacturing their own rifles for many years, but despite this they were all largely similar in design, mechanism and performance, and hadn't really changed too much over the previous twenty years. All used a bolt action and a magazine that allowed for several shots to be fired before reloading. Most variants had a magazine design that was integral to the rifle itself, but some were removable. During the war there was very little advancement in design, as the main manufacturers concentrated on mass-producing reliable weapons rather than experimenting with new designs. Most rifles were approximately 1.25m long and weighed in at around 4kg. Calibres were also very similar across all designs: the 1898 Mauser from Germany had a calibre of 0.312in, the Moisin-Nagant from Russia was 0.3in, British rifles were all 0.303in and American-made weapons came in at 0.3in.

The performance levels of the main rifle designs were also largely similar. Maximum range was about 3,500yd; however for ranges over 600yd a single rifle was unlikely to hit its target consistently. Such ranges required several riflemen firing together at a common target. In a similar fashion, although it was possible for highly trained army regulars to be able to fire off fifteen to twenty rounds per minute – as demonstrated by the British Expeditionary Force during the Battle of Mons in 1914 – 'rapid fire' for the average soldier under battle conditions was typically around eight to twelve rounds per minute.

Any individual that excelled in the art of rifle fire was earmarked for a special role as a sniper. The sniper's role rose to prominence quickly and proved particularly important during static trench warfare. Snipers often worked with a 'spotter', a man equipped with either binoculars or a trench periscope, who identified potential targets. Snipers regularly operated from heavily camouflaged dens, often firing from behind a metal plate with a rifle-sized hole cut into it, in an effort to minimise the risk of injury from any enemy retaliation.

## I WAS THERE

*I saw one man single me out and come at me with his bayonet. He made a lunge at my chest, and, as I guarded, his bayonet glanced aside and wounded me in the hip; but I managed to jab him in the left arm and get him on the ground, and when he was there I hammered him on the head with the butt-end of my rifle.*

*Unidentified private soldier of the King's Own Yorkshire Light Infantry[2]*

**DID YOU KNOW?**

It is alleged that Billy Sing of the 5th Australian Light Horse successfully sniped 150 Turks whilst serving at Gallipolli. As a result he was bestowed a fitting nickname: 'The Murderer'.

As well as a rifle, all infantrymen were issued with a bayonet – a blade that attached to the barrel of the rifle for use in times of close combat. There were three main types of bayonet. The most common were shaped like a blade of a knife, whilst others were much thinner 'needle' types, although these often snapped. Some German troops were issued with bayonets that sported a serrated blade to help with various tasks around the trenches, although British propaganda at the time begged to differ.

Much emphasis was put on what the British described as 'the spirit of the bayonet', and there are many videos and images of soldiers charging sacks of hay and other material with their bayonets during training. The reality in the trenches, however, was very different. Bayonet charges were extremely rare after the initial skirmishes of 1914. The bayonet was more often used for opening tins of food, scraping mud off boots, toasting bread and other mundane purposes than for running through the enemy in bitter hand-to-hand fighting. The fact that British medical staff included bayonet wounds under 'miscellaneous injuries' rather than having a category all to their own suggests that wounds and deaths due to bayoneting were not all that common.

# PISTOLS

IN THE TRENCHES and the front-line areas on all sides of the wire, the handgun was second only to the rifle as the most common personal weapon. Revolvers and automatic pistols were standard issue for all officers, regardless of rank, age or experience. But handguns were not just restricted to the officer class. They were also carried by members of the rank-and-file employed in specialist work or who carried out their duties in an environment that necessitated the carrying of a smaller weapon rather than a long rifle; crews of armoured cars and tanks, aircrew and some miners were among the ordinary men who were allowed to carry a pistol. Also, members of the military police carried sidearms, as they needed to have their hands free to check paperwork and contain prisoners.

At the beginning of 1914 there were three main designs of modern pistol: a common revolver that possessed a rotating chamber, typically of six rounds; a clip-loaded automatic;

### DID YOU KNOW?

The Mauser automatic was probably the most powerful pistol in operation during the war and was popular within the Italian Navy. It had a muzzle velocity of 440m per second.

and the 'blowback' automatic, which used the propellant gas to force the bolt back during firing. In much the same way as the rifle, each main-fighting force of the war manufactured their own handguns, the most iconic of which was perhaps the German-made Luger 9mm. However, it was not made in sufficient numbers to keep up with demand and other German manufacturers like Mauser and Beholla supplied automatic pistols in significant numbers too. All three German variants were exported to Austria-Hungary (although it did have its own Steyr M1911 semi-automatic), Bulgaria and Turkey.

On the British side of the wire, Webley was the wartime pistol manufacturer of choice. They managed to produce 300,000 guns for the war effort, which, despite being a huge output, still wasn't quite enough to meet the needs of the British Armed Forces. Many officers and men of the Royal Navy, Royal Naval Air Service, Royal Flying Corps and Royal Air Force could often be seen sporting US Colt automatics.

The French Army was well served by the 8mm Lebel revolver, which was an accurate and much loved weapon that continued to be used until after the Second World War. The US Army was issued with 0.45in Colt automatics as well as Smith & Wesson sidearms of the same calibre.

## I WAS THERE

*He saw me at exactly the same time as I saw him and he raised his rifle, but he must have been impeded by this overcoat because he couldn't get it up to his shoulder quick enough. I knew jolly well that if he had I should have caught it. It was either him or me. It was the first time I'd ever fired my revolver in anger, so to speak. The first time I'd ever seen a German soldier, apart from prisoners. I killed him with one shot.*

*Second Lieutenant F.W. Beadle, 159th Brigade, Royal Field Artillery[3]*

### DID YOU KNOW?

One particular blowback pistol, the Belgian-made 7.6mm Browning Model 1900, played perhaps the most crucial role in the whole war: it was this weapon that was used by Gavrilo Princip to assassinate Archduke Franz Ferdinand on 28 June 1914.

The Italians had their own manufacturer too; the Glisenti 9mm automatic shared many characteristics of the German-made Luger, but was not as durable and not made in sufficient numbers. Other Italian manufacturers such as Beretta, with their more modern 7.65mm automatic, helped to fill the gap in supply. The Russian Army often struggled to equip its officers and men sufficiently, and the matter of pistols was no exception. Officially, Russian officers were equipped with old Mauser automatics or French Nagant revolvers, but in reality the officers used anything they could get their hands on.

The fact that it was primarily the men of the officer class who carried a pistol instead of a rifle made it easy for snipers and other enemy marksmen to identify and eliminate them. As a consequence, some officers opted for rifles, especially when taking part in an offensive, in an effort to try to blend in with the massed ranks of the infantry. This risk aside, there is no doubt that the revolver played an important role in the war, not just as a useful weapon in the tight confines of a trench, tank, plane or armoured car, but also as an indicator of rank and authority.

# MACHINE GUNS

IF THERE IS one weapon that personifies the First World War it is the machine gun. It was the undisputed king of trench warfare and dominated infantry battles from Ypres to the Vosges Mountains and beyond.

The machine gun of 1914 was quite primitive but was still devastatingly effective. The brightest minds of the German Army calculated that the firepower of one heavy machine gun was equal to that of eighty riflemen. In the harsh environments of trench warfare, it was easy to see why the machine gun was so revered on all sides.

Despite such impressive firepower – a rate of 600 rounds per minute was common – those early heavy machine guns were far from the perfect weapon. Firing at that kind of speed caused the barrel to suffer from severe overheating, often after just a few minutes of firing, and so they needed constant cooling.

### DID YOU KNOW?

The water blanket of the German Maxim heavy machine gun took 7.5 pints of water, which was raised to boiling point after one minute of continuous firing.

## I WAS THERE

*We dashed forward and I found, right in my line of advance, a patch of thistles and nettles. Reaching this, I pushed my Lewis gun through this small, but dense growth of weeds. This afforded complete horizontal cover to my number two with his ammunition, and for my body. Having pushed the gun through and dividing the nettles I found my first target of the day, six or eight Germans in a trench firing at our men stranded in the open. One good burst of fire cleared that parapet.*

*Corporal J. Norton, 8th Battalion, Norfolk Regiment[‡]*

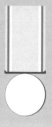

## I WAS THERE

*The German machine gun fire was terrible. Our colonel was hit after only a few steps along the trench. I helped to prop him up against the trench side. Then, we climbed on to the top of the trench. I had not reached my full height when a machine gun bullet smacked into my steel helmet. I felt as if I had been hit with a sledge hammer. I caught a glimpse of my helmet; it was completely smashed in.*

*Private W.H.T. Carter, 1st Bradford Pals Battalion*[5]

Such cooling took one of two forms. Air-cooling used radiating fins attached to the barrel, while in water-cooled systems the barrel was wrapped in a 'water jacket' into which water was poured, acting as a cooling agent. However, often the water was boiling after just a few minutes of firing, plus there was the difficulty of carrying large amounts of water around the battlefield. Whether air-cooled or water-cooled, all guns suffered with frequent jamming, especially in the summer. As such, to ensure a reliable defensive position machine guns would often be grouped together in formation.

These guns were called 'heavy' for a reason. They were primarily weapons of defence, designed to fire on attacking infantry from a fixed position mounted on a tripod; they were not intended for nimble, mobile attacks. Most weighed in the region of 35–45kg and needed a small team of men to get the best out of the gun. Then there was the question of ammunition; a typical British Vickers gun would have had anything up to sixteen ammunition belts, each weighing 10kg, available for immediate use. Keeping one of these heavy guns in use was a serious undertaking. The British Army had a team of six for each heavy machine gun: the number one was the principal gunner, who carried the tripod, mounted and fired the gun and was responsible for direction and elevation. The number two carried the gun and supervised the feed of ammunition, while the number three carried ammunition, number four carried ammunition and also looked after the water jacket, and numbers five and six acted as scouts and range-finders

In attacking situations, gunners were trained to elevate their guns and fire over the heads of their own advancing troops, in an effort to drop the rounds onto enemy positions. However, this was a risky strategy, for obvious reasons.

The light machine gun was developed on all sides during the war and allowed gunners to better keep pace with advancing infantry. Although comparatively light, weighing in at between 10 and 14kg plus ammunition (belts or magazines), they were still heavy machines to haul across the battlefield in the middle of an

### DID YOU KNOW?

Estimates suggest that German machine guns were responsible for 90 per cent of the casualties suffered by the British Army on the first day of the Battle of the Somme.

advance, and the difficulty of supplying sufficient ammunition proved to be a constant problem.

As the war progressed, machine guns were adapted to fit a range of uses. Light machine guns were adapted to be carried on aircraft from 1915 onwards, and became particularly effective with the introduction of interrupter equipment that enabled the gun to be fired through the aircraft's propeller blades. They were also adapted for use on tanks and armoured cars.

# GRENADES

THE POTENTIAL OF the grenade as an effective weapon in close-quarter combat was highlighted in the Russo-Japanese War of 1904–05. Once again it was Germany that got its act together quickest, with the other major nations, including Britain, quite slow to introduce them to the front line. Britain was so slow to get sufficient quantities of reliable grenades to the trenches that front-line soldiers were forced to build improvised grenades out of whatever they could lay their hands on; tin cans full of bits of scrap metal, nails, and barbed wire that acted as shrapnel proved especially useful.

There were two basic types of official grenades: those that were thrown by hand, and those that were projected from a small weapon. Despite the eventual plethora of designs that ended up in front-line trenches, all exhibited the same basic construction: a metal case full of explosives and shrapnel, which ignited on impact (the grenade would explode when it hit something hard) or after a set time.

Time-fuse grenades tended to be more reliable that impact grenades. A number of systems were used to set the timer. Some needed to be tapped on a hard surface to start the timing mechanism, while others used a striker method similar to that of a modern safety match. There were also grenades that

## I WAS THERE

*The English resisted valiantly. Every traverse was contested. Mills Bombs and stick-bombs crossed and recrossed. Behind each we found dead or still quivering bodies.*

*Lieutenant Ernst Jünger, 73rd Hanovarian Fusilier Regiment[6]*

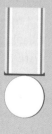

had a safety cord that either hung loosely out of the grenade itself or was looped round the wrist of the thrower and detached automatically when it left the hand. Perhaps the most effective form of time fuse was the spring-loaded activation system, set live when a pin was pulled from the grenade. This system was used in the British Mills bomb (officially designated the No. 5 grenade), which was one of the most common and effective grenades to see active service during the war. The No. 5 was of the classic iron pineapple design with a central striker held by a hand lever that was secured in place by a pin.

The No. 5, like many grenades, had a lethal radius that was greater than the distance it could be thrown. As such, if it was used over open ground it would prove just as dangerous to the thrower as to its intended audience. A competent thrower could achieve a distance of around 15–20m, but when it exploded the No. 5 would scatter pieces of deadly shrapnel over a much wider distance. Because of this the thrower needed to be able to take sufficient cover once he had thrown his weapon. The trench environment often provided perfect cover and grenades were very useful in trench raids and when enemy front-line trenches were close together.

**DID YOU KNOW?**

William Mills, a hand grenade designer from Sunderland, patented, developed and manufactured the 'Mills bomb' at the Mills munitions factory in Birmingham, England, in 1915 and designated it the 'No. 5'. Approximately 75 million grenades were made during the First World War.

In an effort to increase the range that grenades could be thrown, Germany developed the stick grenade, which was first introduced in 1915. The stick provided a lever, which meant a trained thrower could achieve distances of over 30m. To ignite the grenade a cap at the base of the stick was unscrewed to allow a ball and cord to fall out. By pulling the cord the timing fuse was set, giving approximately five seconds to throw the grenade. The downside of the stick design was that it was larger, more cumbersome and fewer could be carried into a fight.

The British Army eventually developed its own specialist grenade teams, known sometimes as 'bombing parties'. This nine-man team consisted of one non-commissioned officer, two designated throwers, two carriers, two bayonet men and two spare men to take over in the case of casualties. In a trench raid

# I WAS THERE

I got up and picked up my rifle and got through the wire into their trench and straight in front there was this dugout – full of Jerries, and one big fellow was on the steps facing me. I had this Mills bomb. Couldn't use my arm. I pulled the pin with my teeth and flung it down and I were shouting at them, I were that wild. 'There you are! Bugger yourselves! Share that between you!'

25884 Private Ernest Deighton, 8th Battalion King's Own Yorkshire Light Infantry[7]

a bombing party such as this would move through an enemy trench, and when they got to a trench bay the two throwers would lob a couple of grenades into the bay. After the explosions had died down the bayonet men would go in to finish off any enemy soldiers who still survived, before issuing a signal to tell the bombers to go on to the next bay.

The business of grenade-throwing was riddled with danger and the incidents of soldiers being badly wounded or killed by their own grenades were numerous. On 22 December 1915, Second Lieutenant Alfred Victor Smith, of the 1/5th Battalion, the East Lancashire Regiment (Territorial Forces), was throwing a grenade, when it slipped from his hand and fell to the bottom of the trench, rolling close to several British officers and men. He shouted and jumped clear, but seeing that the others

### DID YOU KNOW?

The greatest grenade battle of the war undoubtedly took place on Pozières Heights during the night of 26–27 July 1916. For over twelve hours, Australian and British soldiers exchanged grenades with their German enemy. The Allies threw over 15,000 Mills bombs during that night.

could not get into cover he returned without any hesitation and flung himself down onto the grenade. The explosion instantly killed him. He was posthumously awarded the Victoria Cross.

An alternative to the hand grenade was the rifle grenade. Early rifle grenades worked by attaching the bomb to a metal rod that allowed it to be pushed down the barrel of a rifle. By firing a blank round, the grenade would be launched from the rifle. Although this meant a greater distance could be covered, accuracy of fire was often very poor and there were significant safety issues. The grenade had to be primed before launching and if there was a problem firing the rifle immediately it would explode. Continuous firing also caused damage to the rifle barrel. As a result, the majority of front-line troops favoured the simplicity of the hand grenade, despite the potential hazards.

# TRENCH MORTARS

PORTABLE ARTILLERY PIECES that could fire explosive shells at high trajectory had been around for centuries and were a stalwart of siege warfare during the eighteenth century. However, as time passed other methods of waging war became more fashionable and the use of such mortars became almost redundant. It wasn't until the onset of static trench warfare in late 1914 that the main protagonists all realised that these old-style weapons could be very useful. The problem was there were not many about; France had to recommission some nineteenth-century equipment and Britain could only lay its hands on a handful of Japanese mortars with very limited ammunition stocks, as it had none of its own. Germany was in slightly better shape at the beginning of the war, as it had witnessed the usefulness of such weapons in the Russo-Japanese war and had started to design and manufacture some *Minenwerfers*, but even so it couldn't call upon anywhere near the amount it really needed.

### DID YOU KNOW?

The 240mm French Batignolles mortar fired a 192lb bomb that could create a crater 30ft across and 10ft deep.

Early British attempts to plug the gap were somewhat crude improvisations that would not have looked out of place in a medieval castle siege; an example of this was the British Leach catapult, which resembled a large crossbow and was able to throw a 1.5lb grenade up to 200yd.

Contemporary trench mortars began to appear on all sides of the front in decent quantities during 1915. All had a short barrel and many resembled miniature howitzer guns. They all used explosive bombs fitted with fins to aid stability during flight. Effective range for early models varied from 200–500yd.

The Germans continued to develop their *Minenwerfers* throughout the war. They were designed to resemble miniature artillery guns, and because they couldn't be broken down into parts for transportation many required wheeled horse-drawn carriages to move them into position. They could be fired from these carriages if needed, but were usually positioned on a steel firing plate in the trenches. Most of the German mortars had rifled bores to aid accuracy and calibres ranged from 7.6cm to 24.5cm. The smaller mortars were genuinely portable and could be used quite effectively by front-line troops. However, the larger mortars were practically field guns and weighed too much to be a mobile weapon of any use.

## I WAS THERE

When Colonel Donovan called for the Stokes Mortars to repel the threatened counter-attack on the morning of the 15th, the pieces were set up under the slight protection of the sloping ground, but from this point the gunners could not observe the accuracy of their own fire. So Sergeant Fitzsimmons ran forward to the top of the slope, making himself an easy cockshot for the German gunners while he signaled to his own men his corrections on their aim. He escaped himself by a miracle and had the satisfaction of seeing the shells dropping amongst the Germans who were gathering for the attack, and doing dreadful execution.

Frances Patrick Duffy, Military Chaplain, 69th Infantry Regiment, US Army'

Much more portable and manoeuvrable were the grenade mortars (*Granatenwerfer*), which could send a finned grenade up to 300yd. Innovations to the grenade led to the development late in the war of a variant that could bounce. This meant that the grenade would burst in the air like a shrapnel round. On the other end of the scale, the 24cm smooth-bored *Flügelminenwerfer* weighed 3,000lb and was so volatile it had to be fired using a long lanyard.

Allied mortars were all smooth bored. The most common were the French 'Batignolles', which were also used by the USA, Italy and some British troops, and the British Stokes mortar, designed in 1915 and named after its designer Sir Wilfred Stokes. The Stokes was truly portable; it needed a crew of two rather than the *Minenwerfer*'s crew of six. This was because it could be broken down into three sections – the barrel, baseplate and bipod mount – and assembled easily in situ. It also had an automatic ignition, which meant that a bomb could be dropped into the tube and ejected immediately. Different sizes of the Stokes were used for different types of ammunition. The smaller 3in mortars were primarily used for high explosives and smoke bombs, while the 4in and 6in mortars were used for gas shells and incendiary bombs, as well as some smoke bombs.

# FLAMETHROWERS

GERMANY HAD BEEN testing both static and portable flamethrowers as a viable weapon from as early as 1900, and had actually set up three specialist battalions specifically trained to use them in 1911. Both versions of the flamethrower used pressurised air to force oil or petrol through a nozzle, which, once ignited by a spark, transformed into a jet of flame.

There were two German variants of a portable flamethrower: the 'Kleif' and the 'Wex'. The Kleif (*Kleinflammenwerfer*) or small flamethrower was not especially small at all and needed two men to work it; one carried the fuel container on his back and the other aimed and fired the nozzle. The Kleif had an effective range of some 25m and they were often deployed in groups of six to help attacking infantry clear enemy trenches of defenders. The Wex (*Wechselapparat*) was smaller and operated by just one man, wearing a container of fuel on his back. Even so, the tactical use of such weapons was limited to small skirmishes, convincing enemy soldiers to surrender or evacuate their dugouts, attacking strongpoints

**DID YOU KNOW?**
During the war it is estimated that Germany launched over 650 separate flamethrower attacks.

and covering retreating infantry after trench raids or other attacks.

The first notable use of flamethrowers came during a surprise German attack near Hooge. The British troops who were on the receiving end of this attack were terrified and immediately surrendered their position, although their defensive line was later consolidated and strengthened to limit the German advance. In two days of fighting the British lost just under 800 men. After this initial success the German High Command instigated a wider adoption of flamethrowers. There can be no denying they were incredibly useful during an offensive in a close combat situation, despite the risks posed to the operators – they were very often targeted with concentrated fire, due to both the amounts of potentially explosive fuel they carried and the fact they were generally despised by the enemy. If any flame operators were taken prisoner they would not have had a pleasant time. It was a very dangerous existence.

France was the other major belligerent to get in on the act early with portable flamethrowers. The French version was deployed into the front-line trenches from 1917 onwards. It was called the Schilt, after its inventor and, like the Wex, was carried on the back of a single crewman.

# I WAS THERE

Working down gradually I decided to go on along the stretch of trench which bent back from the German line almost in the form of a communication trench. There were servants and some odd men from my platoon in so called 'shelters' along there, and I wanted to make sure that these people who are apt to be forgotten at 'stand-to' were all on the alert. Just as I was getting to the last of these there was a hissing sound, and a bright crimson glare over the crater turned the whole scene red. As I looked I saw three or four distinct jets of flame, like a line of powerful fire-hoses spraying fire instead of water, shoot across my fire trench. For some moments I was utterly unable to think. Then there was a terrific explosion and almost immediately afterwards one of my men with blood running down his face stumbled into me coming from the direction of the crater. Then every noise under Heaven broke out.

Second Lieutenant G.V. Carey, 8th Battalion, Rifle Brigade[2]

It boasted slightly better performance than the German Wex, as it was able to carry more fuel (3 gallons as opposed to 2.75 gallons for the Wex) and had a greater range.

The British did design a couple of different variations of portable flamethrower, the Norris-Menchen and the Lawrence. However, apart from a cameo appearance during the raid on Zeebrugge in 1918, neither variation was used in anger.

The heavier versions of these flamethrowers were set up as cylinders of gas set into defensive strongpoints and emplacements. The German version was called the 'Grof' (*Grossflamenwerfer*, meaning 'large flamethrower') and had a range of effective fire of up to 40m over a duration of forty seconds, but was really only useful for defending the positions into which it was set.

The British had a go at designing their own large flamethrower. The Livens, once more named after its inventor, was designed to be operated from a dugout and could deliver huge amounts of burning flame over a three- or four-minute period. The main problem with these heavy flamethrowers was the fuel needed to keep the flame burning. For example, to keep thirty Livens flamethrowers working would require 1,000 gallons of petrol per minute, a

## I WAS THERE

*I decided to go on along the stretch of trench which bent back from the German line almost in the form of a communication trench. There were servants and some odd men from my platoon in so-called 'shelters' along there, and I wanted to make sure these people who are adapt to be forgotten at 'stand-to' were all on alert. Just as I was getting to the last of these there was a sudden hissing sound, and a bright crimson glare over the crater turned the whole scene red. As I looked I saw three or four distinct jets of flame, like a line of powerful fire-hoses spraying fire instead of water, shoot across my fire trench. For some moments I was utterly unable to think.*

*Second Lieutenant G.V. Carey, 8th Battalion, Rifle Brigade[10]*

quantity of fuel that was simply not available at the front line.

By the end of the war, many tanks had also been fitted with flamethrower equipment, a trend that was continued in the Second World War.

# GAS

GAS HAD BEEN considered by all belligerents as a serious weapon of war for years before the breakout of hostilities in 1914, but the general consensus on all sides was that it was not a chivalrous weapon and as such it was never used in anger.

With the onset of trench warfare, and the massive amount of human loss that was mounting up on a daily basis, Generals on all sides were getting desperate for a way of breaking the deadlock of trench warfare and so revisited the subject of gas as a viable offensive weapon.

It was in fact the French that first used gas (they threw crude tear-gas grenades at the Germans in August 1914), but it was the Germans who managed to figure out the finer details of large-scale gas warfare first. Their first couple of attempts, at Neuve Chapelle on the Western Front in October 1914 and then again in January 1915 on the Eastern Front near Bolimov, were not very successful due to adverse weather.

### DID YOU KNOW?

Germany was the most prolific user of gas during the war. It produced and used more than 68,000 tonnes, compared with the 37,000 tonnes used by France and the 25,000 tonnes used by Great Britain.

## I WAS THERE

*Gas shelling began. Those sinister shells which land with a harmless snuffed sound, like duds, but soon poison the air. The men adjusted box respirators, but a good many were too late and went away with splotched and streaming faces.*

*Lieutenant Carroll Carstairs MC, Grenadier Guards[11]*

Early gas strategy relied on the poison gas being released towards the enemy trenches from large cylinders that were positioned near to the front line. This procedure was very reliant on the wind blowing the gas in the right direction, but often the wind could drop, leaving the gas hanging over no-man's-land, or even worse change direction, blowing the gas back on its own line.

In April 1915, during the Second Battle of Ypres, the German Army got the tactics for gas warfare correct, with devastating results. After releasing large amounts of chlorine gas in the direction of the French line, the Germans attacked and advanced a mile through broken lines, with hardly a shot being fired. Suddenly gas was a viable weapon that threatened to put an end to the stalemate of trench warfare, and all sides got busy developing their own gas strategy.

Gases were generally split into two groups: lethal and irritant. Lethal gas, such as the numerous cyanogen compounds used by the Allies from 1916, caused instant death. Irritants were not quite so deadly but could still cause significant suffering and debilitation. The most common gases encountered across the front line were chlorine and mustard gas. Chlorine was a harsh irritant that targeted

## I WAS THERE

Clouds of gas blew backwards and we had to tuck our helmets which we were wearing all the tighter. I was wearing two helmets one over the other, but in spite of these my throat became very sore. Even before we started one of the gas men in the traverse in which I was standing keeping an eye on my watch became overcome while working his removal sprayer and was lying at my feet groaning horribly. I was counting the seconds and when I gave the signal to cross the parapet I think we were all glad to get out of our trench full of gas. The air in front was thick with gas and smoke from the smoke bombs and we couldn't see more than a few yards.

Captain W.G. Bagot-Chester MC, 2/3rd Gurkha Rifles[12]

the respiratory system, causing vomiting and, if inhaled in large enough quantities, could be fatal. Mustard gas was one of the most effective gases used. Although not technically lethal, it was very nasty. It blistered and burnt the skin, even when clothes were worn, and if inhaled would case massive internal bleeding that usually led to death.

From 1916, artillery shells were widely used as an alternative vehicle to deliver gas, rather than just relying on the wind to blow clouds of it over the enemy lines. They were modified to carry liquid gas that evaporated on explosion. Using artillery shells to deposit gas increased the range and accuracy of delivery, but despite these obvious advantages, gas never became the war-winning weapon that the Generals wished. Even when being used as part of an artillery bombardment, the gas needed the correct weather conditions (wind, temperature and humidity) in order to be effective. In addition, all sides had quickly developed gas masks to negate the effects of any gas attack.

### DID YOU KNOW?

An early recommendation for effective protection from gas was to hold a urine-soaked handkerchief over mouth and nose.

Early gas masks consisted of nothing more than a pair of goggles and a piece of cloth soaked in chemicals that could be placed over mouth and nose, but as the war progressed gas protection became more sophisticated, culminating in the full face mask with respirator that has become an image synonymous with the First World War. By 1916 even horses and mules had specially designed respirators to help them stave off the effects of gas.

# ARMOURED CARS

THE FIRST RECOGNISABLE armoured cars started to appear just after the turn of the twentieth century, less than twenty years after the appearance of the first petrol-driven vehicles. Most of the vehicles at this time were nothing more than civilian cars with bits of armour plate bolted to the sides and the roof. They were very bespoke and experimental in nature, put together using whatever raw materials were to hand. The vast majority of them had normal wheels and ran on normal tyres. Only a few Russian vehicles sported half-tracks to enable them to go off-road. Not surprisingly, only a small number of them ever found their way anywhere near a live battlefield.

As the years rolled by, the design and development of armoured cars improved. They were mostly manufactured by civilian car-makers; Rolls-Royce, Lanchester and Wolseley were the main producers in Britain, with Daimler and Ehrhardt making similar cars in Germany, Peugeot and Renault working in France and Fiat and Lancia in Italy. Before the war, early uses of the armoured car were for intelligence gathering, scouting and reconnaissance, launching fast ambushes and counter-attacks and pursuing a fleeing enemy. They were most effective in a mobile war over relatively flat terrain and did make a number of

**DID YOU KNOW?**

The Canadian Automobile Machine Gun Brigade was the first fully mechanised unit in the history of the British Army. The brigade was established on 2 September 1914 in Ottawa, as Automobile Machine Gun Brigade No. 1 by Brigadier General Raymond Brutinel.

effective appearances in the early skirmishes of the First World War, before the race to the sea and the onset of static trench warfare. Many of these cars were very heavy because of all their armour, and they were often badly underpowered by their primitive engines. Traction and grip were also poor and the cars were defeated by even the slightest muddy slope in the smashed grounds of the Western Front. Range Rovers these were definitely not. The armour wasn't up to the job either. It was ok with rifle and small arms fire, but didn't stand a chance against any kind of artillery. Armament was typically a number of light machine guns, but some carried heavier cannon.

It was obvious that further development was needed if armoured cars were going to play any significant part in the war. The Royal Naval

## I WAS THERE

*2 Armoured Cars were ordered forward
to cooperate with and assist "A" and "B"
Batteries, which had been instructed to advance
towards Bossu. In spite of what appeared to be a
favourable opportunity for the employment of
mobile forces, the advance of the Armoured Cars
and Batteries was completely stopped by a huge
Mine Crater ...*

*Canadian Automobile Machine Gun Brigade, unit diary,
7 November 1918[13]*

Air Service led the way in innovation when it started to request purpose-built cars to help with the rescue of shot-down pilots and report on the movement of the enemy. As these journeys became more and more dangerous, the need for professionally designed armoured vehicles became ever more urgent. The request for 'fighting cars' was given to Rolls-Royce and by the end of 1914 the first vehicles arrived in the fighting zone. Unfortunately by then the Western Front had bogged down into a static war not really suited to mobile vehicles. After the development of tracked tanks in 1916 to overcome the terrain issue, the use of armoured cars was restricted to areas such as Palestine and Mesopotamia where the ground was flatter, and here they performed a cavalry role of pursuit with great aplomb. It was not until the resumption of a more mobile war in 1918 that the armoured car made an impact on the Western Front.

Despite these obvious limitations, each major belligerent got in on the act of producing its own armoured cars. Some were fully enclosed with armoured roofs, while others were more open to the elements (and enemy bullets), and armament ranged from a single machine gun up to small-calibre cannons. One of the most competent armoured vehicles was the German

Panzerkraftwagen Ehrhardt, which boasted an engine that produced 85bhp (the first Rolls-Royce cars had 50bhp), had a top speed of almost 40mph, could carry a crew of eight or nine over a range of over 150 miles and packed three machine guns.

# BRITISH TANKS

IN AUTUMN 1914, the landscape of Flanders hadn't yet succumbed to the merciless pounding of the guns and farmers still harvested their crops and went about their normal business. It was, among other things, the sight of some of this agricultural machinery that got a few of the clever chaps from the British Expeditionary Force thinking. Wouldn't it be a great idea if they could have an armoured, motorised gun to support the infantry when things got a bit frantic in the field? It would be even better if the aforementioned gun could be loaded onto the caterpillar tracks used for some farm equipment, to allow easier movement across a wider variety of terrain.

A formal memorandum on 'special devices' was compiled in December 1914, in which such equipment was officially mentioned for the first time. Simultaneously the Royal Navy was working on similar ideas. The naval minister,

**DID YOU KNOW?**

The tank made its operational debut on 15 September 1916 during the Battle of Flers-Courcelette.

a certain Winston Churchill, having read the army report and being aware of the navy ideas, put together a Technical Landship Committee (taken from the navy's code name for them) in February 1915.

In June that year the committee had formulated their technical 'want' list. They demanded a land speed of 4mph, 'rapid' all-round manoeuvrability, a range of 12 miles and some big guns, all bolted to a caterpillar track. After seeing a wooden mock-up in September, Sir Douglas Haig, Commander-in-Chief of the British Expeditionary Force, was impressed enough to order forty and went off dreaming of these new machines ripping through the German defences with ease, scattering the enemy and destroying their positions. Prime Minster Lloyd George approved the project and production started in April 1916.

Imaginatively named after their coded transportation name of 'water tanks', the first batch of Mark I tanks entered service with the Heavy Section of the Machine Gun Corps, later to become the Tank Corps, in June 1916, although they had to wait until the middle of September before they saw active service for the first time. Tactics and strategy were mulled over for months during the run-up to the big day. In the end, Haig, going against the advice of his field officers, decided to mass all forty-nine serviceable tanks in an attack on a limited objective during the Battle of Flers-Courcelette. The press had a field day, with wild reports of masses of Germans soldiers running for their lives at the sight of these metal monsters and being squashed by the huge metal tracks.

The reality, however, was a little different. Although the sight of the tanks did cause a good deal of confusion in the German lines, only a few of the tanks were able to advance any meaningful distance, due to some technical gremlins. Firstly the crews were not properly trained. Then there is the fact that the tanks themselves were not properly tested due to the rush to get them into the field. As a consequence, they were mechanically very unreliable in action, with many breaking down before they got anywhere near the enemy lines. The crew had practically zero visibility and were forced to rely on messages tapped on the hulls of the tanks by the infantrymen. Conditions inside them were also difficult. If the crew were not poisoned by the engine fumes, then they were slowly boiled by the insane heat inside the cabin. If they survived that lot, then there was always the possibility of being burnt to a crisp in a fireball after either being hit by the enemy, or just because of a random act of sudden incineration.

# I WAS THERE

*Inside, above the noise of the engine, was heard the sharp cracking of our own machine guns, mingled with the groaning and whining of the gunner who lay stretched along the blood and oil saturated floor; this, with the vomiting of our second driver, intense heat, exhaust petrol fumes, and mauseous [sic] vapour from the guns made an inferno that no outside observer would have thought possible to exist within those steel plates.*

*305851 Private Arthur Jenkins, Tank Corps*[14]

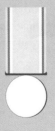

Despite all this, the British High Command saw something in the tank that gave them hope of ultimate victory and ordered more. Subsequent new versions were much improved. The Mark IV had thicker armour to help protect the crew against German armour-piercing bullets. The Mark V saw power upped to 150bhp and sported innovations such as an epicyclic gear system, which enabled it to be steered by just one man. As well as these heavy tanks, a smaller, lighter and faster tank was produced, called the Whippet, designed to capitalise on gaps in the enemy line. It had a heady top speed of 8mph and made its operational debut in 1918. Alongside heavy Mark IV and V tanks, the Whippet took part in the Amiens offensive of 8 August 1918, breaking through to the German rear and causing havoc with their artillery placements across a huge area of the front.

### DID YOU KNOW?

There were two variants of the British heavy tank: a 'male', which had two 6-pounder guns and three 8mm Hotchkiss machine guns, and a 'female', which had one 6-pounder gun and four machine guns.

Successes like Amiens, and that at the first day of the Battle of Cambrai in late 1917, sealed the (positive) fate of the tank in future British offensives. However, partly due to continued design weaknesses and reliability issues, as well as poor tactics, the tank was reduced to being only a bit-part player in the overall Allied victory.

# FRENCH AND
# GERMAN TANKS

INDEPENDENTLY OF BRITAIN and its Landship Committee, France was also working on a range of armoured, tracked vehicles, and a number of officials in the French Ministry of War also thought that these vehicles could hold the key to unlocking the Western Front. Early design and activity in this area was fronted by an artillery man, Colonel Jean-Baptise Estienne, who put together a concept in December 1915, which was quickly accepted, and an initial order for 400 was issued in January 1916. A major arms manufacturer, Schneider, was the first to try to produce something useable and based their first design on a US tractor chassis. It had a top speed of 5mph, weighed 13 tonnes and was equipped with a 75mm Schneider cannon and two Hotchkiss machine guns. The company struggled to keep up with the demands of the French Army due to shortages in raw materials, especially armour plating. By November 1916 there were only a handful of Schneider CA1 in operation when there should have been 400.

To fill the gap, a rival manufacturer, Saint-Chamond, was asked to step up and help with supplying the tanks the army badly needed. It initially wanted to make the same tank as Schneider, but Schneider wouldn't share its designs for free, so Saint-Chamond went ahead with its own design for a bigger, heavier tank with much more firepower in the form of a 75mm field gun and four machine guns.

Despite the rivalry of the two manufacturers, neither tank performed very well in action. They were very unreliable, vulnerable to enemy artillery fire due to their upright design and struggled to cross even the smallest of trenches – a severe disadvantage on the Western Front. Not surprisingly, they were both superseded by a new lighter tank made by Renault. The FT-17 was operational from the end of 1917 and was used extensively by both French and American forces. It was a revolutionary design, as it was the first tank to have a rotating gun turret and separate compartments for crew and engine. Modern tanks of the twenty-first century still copy this basic design.

### DID YOU KNOW?

The first tank-against-tank combat in history took place on 24 April 1918 when three A7Vs taking part in an attack with infantry incidentally met three Mark IVs (two female tanks and one male) near Villers-Bretonneux. During the battle, tanks on both sides were damaged.

# I WAS THERE

Suddenly, against our steel wall, a hurricane of hail pattered, and the interior was filled with myriads of sparks and flying splinters. Something rattled against the steel helmet of the driver sitting next to me and my face was stung with minute fragments of steel.

The crew flung themselves flat on the floor. The driver ducked his head and drove straight on. Above the roar of our engine could be heard the staccato rat-tat-tat-tat of machine guns and another furious jet of bullets sprayed our steel side, the splinters clanging viciously against the engine cover.

The Jerry tank had treated us to a broadside of armour-piercing bullets!

Lieutenant F. Mitchell, 1st Battalion, Tank Corps[15]

The first time the Renault FT-17 tank saw active service was on 31 May 1918, during the Second Battle of the Marne. It was a complete success and by the end of the war over 3,000 FT-17 tanks had been manufactured and shipped to the front.

The German High Command, on the other hand, was much slower to jump on the tank bandwagon. It was concerned that the high rate of mechanical failure and the general fragility of tanks in the front line meant they would just be a lumbering liability to the war effort. That said, the A7V *Panzerkampfwagen* did find its way to the front line in late 1917. It was a monster of a vehicle, measuring over 7m long and weighing over 30 tonnes. The A7V needed a crew of sixteen and was armed with six 7.92mm MG08 machine guns and a 57mm heavy cannon. It was powered by two 100hp Daimler engines that gave it a top speed of around 9mph on roads

**DID YOU KNOW?**

The 1st US Light Tank Brigade, commanded by George S. Patton, was made up entirely of Renault FT tanks.

but only 3mph across country. The A7V made its operational debut on 21 March 1918, just north of the St Quentin Canal, but over front-line terrain they proved ponderously slow. This lack of speed, coupled with poor balance and chronic unreliability, meant that only a tiny number every saw active service. The majority of 'German' tanks involved in fighting were in fact captured and refurbished British models.

# MINES

ALTHOUGH TRENCH WARFARE is synonymous with the First World War, military mining played a significant and often spectacular part too. The idea of digging underneath strongly held fortifications was not a new idea and had been part of siege warfare for centuries. However, with the static nature of front-line trenches and the introduction of high explosives during the war, mining and tunneling took on a whole new dimension.

Mine warfare during the First World War was all about digging deep shafts underneath the enemy trench systems, packing chambers full of high explosives and detonating the charges. Often the explosion was timed to coincide with an infantry attack, as large mines could wipe out entire sections of the enemy line and make it a bit easier for the attacking infantry to consolidate new positions.

Tunnelling underneath the front line was an incredibly dangerous occupation and was the sole responsibility of specialist tunneling companies, who were part of the Royal Engineers. These companies were full of miners and the clay-kickers who worked on the London Underground and national sewerage systems. Clay-kicking was a method of excavating clay where the 'kicker' sat facing the tunnel face, their back supported by a wooden back-rest,

## I WAS THERE

*I saw the effect of the mines. I saw the crater at La Boisselle. It really petrified me, the size of it. I mean, it was as big as a cathedral.*

*Corporal Reginald Leonard Haine, 1st Battalion, Honourable Artillery Company[16]*

and kicked the blade of his spade into the clay, which was then removed by a colleague and passed back for disposal. The work was slow – It could take up to a year of constant digging to get a mine ready for blowing – and it had to be carried out in absolute silence so that the enemy couldn't pinpoint their location. The stress and the conditions were terrible. It was also incredibly dangerous: tunnel collapses, flooding, gas and the ever-present danger of being found by the enemy and subsequently blown to pieces were constant threats to the army of tunnellers who lived and worked below the lines. Once a tunnel was completed and the explosives were all packed in place, a wire fuse was run back out of the tunnel to a plunger/detonator.

The first time British mines were detonated was at Hill 60 on the Ypres salient in April 1915. Ten thousand pounds of explosives were packed in underneath the hill, and when they were detonated on 17 April tons of Flanders mud, sandbags, trench timbers and broken German bodies were flung hundreds of feet into the air. The British attackers rushed for the crater and completely overran the enemy, with minimal casualties. Following on from this success the British High Command was very keen to expand the mining operations up and down the Western Front. The opening salvos of the

Battle of the Somme in July 1916 were preceded by the detonating of seventeen separate mines, the largest of which used a combined charge of 54,000lb of ammonal (the most powerful explosive then known), threw debris 1,200m in the air and produced a crater that was almost 100m across and 30m deep. However, that was nothing compared to what was being planned for the Messines Ridge in 1917.

Digging had started along a 10-mile stretch of the ridge in the summer of 1915 and over the years and months these tunnels were drawn out and extended, culminating in over 8,000m of deep tunnels, packed with twenty-one separate mines that held over 400 tonnes of ammonal. At 3.10 a.m. on 7 June 1917, nineteen mines were detonated (two failed to go off).

The eruption was so colossal it destroyed an estimated 10,000 Germans instantly and was clearly heard in London and other parts

**DID YOU KNOW?**

At the height of the mining activity under the Messines Ridge there were about 20,000 British, Canadian, Australian and New Zealand tunnellers employed in digging deadly holes in the Ridge, with about as many Germans tunneling straight towards them.

of southern England. The largest crater, Lone Tree, was formed by a single mine that housed 91,000lb of ammonal and caused a crater 12m deep and 76m across. It was privately purchased by Lord Wakefield after the war and transformed into the 'Pool of Peace' as an example of mankind's destructiveness. The Pool is now a memorial owned by the Talbot House (Toc H) Museum in Poperinghe, Belgium.

# AIRSHIPS

THE IDEA OF using airships in warfare had been around for a number of years, but it wasn't until the outbreak of the First World War in 1914 that they were used regularly.

In the early years of the war, airships weren't used solely by Germany; both Italy and France used their own airships for reconnaissance and for small-scale tactical bombing raids. However, all sides quickly realised that airships were too slow and too vulnerable to explosives to be of any real use in front-line operations, and by 1917 the role of the airship was exclusively that of bombing.

Perhaps the most iconic airship of the war was designed by Count Graf Zeppelin around the turn of the century and entered military service in March 1909. The Zeppelins had a metal frame and used a series of different internal 'pockets' filled with hydrogen. The crew and other loads, such as bombs, were carried in gondolas that hung underneath. Early Zeppelins measured around 158m long, could travel at about 45mph and needed a crew of sixteen men. As the war advanced, so too did the design of the Zeppelin, gradually getting bigger and faster, with a higher flight altitude, culminating in the 'Super-Zeppelin' of 1916 which nudged 200m long and, with the help of six Maybach engines, could zip along at around 60mph. These Super-Zeppelins needed 55,000m³ of gas to get them off the ground.

Zeppelins were not the only variety of airships. The German Naval Airship Division operated eight airships of the Shütte-Lanz design (smaller than the Zeppelins and with a wooden frame), as well as fifty-nine Zeppelins and six of other types. By March 1915 Paris was putting up with frequent bombing raids and the first attack on London took place on 31 May the same year. Over the course of the war these airships made 1,191 reconnaissance flights and 342 bombing raids.

The bombing raids did cause alarm within the civilian population; the image of gigantic, slow-moving craft sneaking up silently under cover of darkness to wreak havoc on unsuspecting British towns and cities did much to enhance a sinister reputation. However, in reality the airships were a big disappointment to the German High Command. Yes they offered reasonably effective bombing capabilities, but many crashed due to bad weather such as high winds and ice, whilst others were shot down by ground fire or Allied fighter planes equipped with incendiary rockets. They were simply not reliable enough and too vulnerable to be effective.

# I WAS THERE

*... there was a sudden crackle of anti-aircraft gunfire, and simultaneously a dreadful sound that London knew only too well – a sound like no other on earth. It was the mournful wail created by the velocity of a descending bomb. In the one brief terrible moment before the impact I instinctively knew it was coming directly where we stood. I was not wrong. It exploded three yards from where we were standing. It flung me against the wall next to the pit entrance to the Strand theatre... I felt unhurt; only dazed. Yet I had twenty-two lumps of shrapnel embedded in me.*

*James Wickham , call boy at the Gaiety Theatre, London*[17]

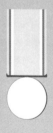

**DID YOU KNOW?**

The largest German airship raid on England took place on the night of 2 September and involved fourteen airships. Between them they dropped 261 high explosive and 202 incendiary bombs over the east of the country. Although little damage was sustained there were four civilian deaths and a dozen injuries.

That said, the Germans persevered with bombing operations, and on the night of 2 September they launched what would be the largest airship raid on Britain during the war. Sixteen airships of various sizes and designs headed towards Britain and although two had to turn back early the rest managed to drop 261 high explosive and 202 incendiary bombs up and down the east coast of England.

By late 1917 airships had largely been replaced by planes and the remaining airships of Germany's fleet were either mothballed or destroyed. A few were handed over after the war as part of the armistice terms. The British airship programme, which at its height operated over 220 non-rigid blimps for scouting and reconnaissance, was also wound down towards the end of the war.

# FIGHTER AIRCRAFT

IN 1914 THE notion of air-to-air combat simply didn't exist. The few planes that each air force had were designed and used for air reconnaissance only; there was nothing purpose-built for blasting enemy machines out of the sky. However, once the trench systems of the Western Front had stabilised and all sides found themselves trying to gain aerial dominance over a relatively small sector of sky, the notion of eliminating enemy machines became more and more important.

In those early days 'fighter planes' were nothing more than reconnaissance planes that had been fitted with a single machine gun, often operated by the observer from the rear of the cockpit. To be effective as a fighter, a plane needed the gun pointing forwards. However, because of the propeller being at the front

### DID YOU KNOW?

The Royal Flying Corps decided not to issue pilots with parachutes because it thought that this would encourage them to bail out of their distressed plane rather than try to bring it home safely.

of the plane there was a very real danger of it being blown to pieces by the aforementioned machine gun. To overcome this a number of solutions were tried out. High-firing machine guns placed above the cockpit and 'pusher' airplanes with the propeller at the back of the plane were tried, but both were very unsatisfactory. In the spring of 1915 a French pilot, Roland Garros, fitted steel plates over the wooden propeller of his Morane-Saulnier two-seater monoplane. By doing this the machine gun bullets were simply deflected off of the steel plating, keeping the propeller intact. Garros trialled this new system on 1 April 1915. It was an immediate success, shooting down an enemy two-seater reconnaissance plane almost immediately. Subsequent victories quickly followed, and the fighter plane was born.

Garros was shot down over German lines on 19 April and before he was able to destroy his machine he was captured and the plane was delivered to the aircraft manufacturer Fokker, with the instruction to make a similar system for German planes. Within forty-eight hours Fokker delivered an Eindecker monoplane fitted with interrupter gear, a device that stopped the machine gun firing when the propeller blade passed in front of its barrel. After initial scepticism from German officers, German pilot

## I WAS THERE

*I saw [the black Albatross machine] start to smoke as I pounded a long burst into it, and then the observer tried to scramble over into the pilot's seat, and the whole lot went up in flames and screwed down out of the mess.*

*A.G.J. Whitehouse, aerial gunner and observer, Royal Flying Corps[18]*

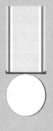

Oswald Boelcke made his first kill using this system on 1 August 1915. This technological leap forward handed the aerial initiative well and truly to the Germans, who dominated the skies over the Western Front in what became known as the 'Fokker Scourge'. It wasn't until the spring of 1916 that the Allies were able to introduce the next generation of their fighters and redress the balance, although these were yet again outclassed in the autumn of 1916 by the new German D-Type fighters. Once again the Allies were losing pilots and planes at an alarming rate; 'Bloody April' 1917 saw the Royal Flying Corps decimated, with 245 aircraft lost and over 300 crew killed or taken prisoner.

The truth is that no one side maintained dominance of the skies for very long until the later stages of the war, when the Allies had the distinct advantage of being able to manufacture much larger numbers of machines than Germany, whose resources and allies were running low.

The development of the forward-firing machine gun coupled with the interrupter gear saw the emergence of different plane designs for different roles. Fighters were now being purpose-built rather than just being modified scout planes, and they were pooled together into specialist fighter squadrons such as the

German Jagdstaffel 11 (No. 11 Fighter Squadron), which boasted a certain Manfred von Richtoffen – commonly referred to as The Red Baron and who was to become the most famous air ace of the First World War – among its commanding officers. Fighters started working together in formation, working together to sniff out enemy machines or protecting less agile bomber craft of reconnaissance planes.

As the fighter plane established itself as a genuine weapon of attack, the notion of the 'fighter ace' was born. All pilots religiously recorded their successes and any pilot who achieved five 'kills' was recognised as an 'ace'. Such men were lauded as heroes in their homeland, being regarded as brave pioneers of modern warfare. This may have been true in some respect but the idealism and romanticism associated with being a fighter pilot was way off the mark. The stark reality was that these men took to the skies in flimsy and unreliable machines that offered little protection from either the elements or the enemy and possessed precious little in terms of safety systems. In 1917 the average life expectancy upon becoming a British pilot was eleven days.

# ANTI-AIRCRAFT GUNS

AT THE OUTBREAK of war no one was really taking anti-aircraft strategies very seriously, and not surprisingly there were very few guns around in 1914. Germany was the first nation to start experimenting with anti-aircraft weapons and in 1909 started to convert a number of field guns to enable them to fire at high angle from a truck. By 1914 there were a small number in service at the front, but because there were so few planes around no country was investing a great deal of time and effort in devising ways of shooting them out of the sky. In those early days infantry soldiers would fire their rifles and machine guns at any plane that buzzed about overhead, with occasional success.

The rapid expansion and development of the air war from 1915 forced the hands of the main nations to invest significantly in developing methods for the strategic and systematic destruction of enemy aircraft. Many artillery guns were quickly modified to perform a role in anti-aircraft defence. Britain, for example, modified a light field gun, originally used within their horse-drawn artillery batteries, so it could fit on the back of trucks. The guns were fitted with stabilisers to prevent the recoil of the guns rolling the vehicle it was strapped to. Such guns could fire a shell at an angle of around 80 degrees up to an altitude of 4,000m.

### DID YOU KNOW?

British soldiers had a number of nicknames for anti-aircraft guns, including 'archies' and 'ack-ack guns', the latter taken from the Western Front version of the army phonetic alphabet for 'AA'. The Germans commonly used the term 'Flak', which was an abbreviation of *Flugzeugabwehrkanone* or aircraft defence cannon.

Germany followed the British lead, mainly modifying its 75mm and 80mm weapons, whereas France used its famous *soixante-quinze* as the basis for its anti-aircraft weapons. As the war continued there wasn't a great deal of technological advancement in terms of gun design. Some guns used lighter shells that increased the range of fire and Germany developed a quick-firing 20mm cannon during 1918, which would eventually become the model for its Second World War light anti-aircraft weapons.

For all nations except Germany, the deployment of anti-aircraft guns was viewed as the responsibility of the artillery. The German guns were run by the German Army Air Service. Initially all countries' anti-aircraft batteries were deployed in small clusters to enable their fire to follow the path of the aircraft they were shooting. At least two guns were used, one to fire a ranging shot that could then be followed very quickly with a more accurate shell form the second gun. This system failed to shoot down many enemy machines and eventually anti-aircraft defences were grouped together in larger numbers, especially around strategic areas such as supply centres, airfields and transport hubs, which were becoming increasingly targeted by strategic bombers.

The biggest problem for any anti-aircraft was trying to accurately target a remote machine that could relatively easily move out the way of any oncoming shell. In an effort to counter this, 'barrage' techniques were implemented, which aimed to cover a particular piece of airspace with fire in an attempt to trap an oncoming machine. There were also improvements in sights and telescopic tracking systems to enable the guns to fire at an anticipated position in front of the target aircraft. For night operations flares and searchlights were used, as well as barrage balloons, which were launched in the air to try to funnel hostile machines into a corridor of airspace that was well covered by anti-aircraft fire.

Most anti-aircraft crews used shrapnel shells for maximum effect, although some high-explosive shells were also used, as these had

# I WAS THERE

*The whole way down I was under fire, two anti-aircraft guns in the yard, guns from the forts on either side, rifle fire, mitrailleuse or machine guns and, most weird of all, great bunches (15 to 20) of what looked like green rockets, but I think they were flaming bullets. The excitement of the moment was terrific. I have never travelled so fast before in my life. My chief impressions were the great speed, the flaming bullets streaking by, the incessant rattle of machine gun rifle fire, and one or two shells bursting close by, knocking my machine all sideways, and pretty nearly deafening me.*

*Flight Lieutenant Harold Rosher, Royal Naval Air Service*[19]

the power to blow a machine out of the sky if they were lucky enough to score a direct hit. By 1918 thermite shells, which behaved in a similar way to shrapnel shells but threw out balls of liquid fire, were also popular.

Despite all the efforts of the anti-aircraft crew and commanders, the reality was that technology in this area was very much in its infancy and was not really capable of making much of an impact in the air war. Anti-aircraft batteries may have been a nuisance to enemy pilots and could put off potential bombing raids, but they only contributed a small amount to overall air casualties.

# DREADNOUGHTS

THE FUTURE OF naval warfare was turned on its head in December 1906 when HMS *Dreadnought* was completed after a record fourteen-month construction period. In the blink of an eye every other battleship that was sailing the seas was suddenly rendered obsolete, such was the radical nature of the design and engineering of this new warship. HMS *Dreadnought* was such a watershed moment in battleship design that a whole new design of ship, built in the years immediately after 1906 and based on her initial construction, were all called 'Dreadnoughts' and older battleships were now referred to as pre-Dreadnoughts.

HMS *Dreadnought* had two major design differences that set her apart from pre-Dreadnought battleships: bigger guns and better engines. She was the first 'all-big-gun' battleship and boasted ten massive 12in guns, as opposed to just four 12in guns as a main battery and smaller 6in guns in a secondary battery. The all-big-gun design had a number of advantages over the old design. The obvious advantage was an improved range and intensity of long-range fire, but on top of this there were numerous improvements to the running of the ship too. Having all of the guns firing the same calibre shell meant simpler logistics in terms of supplying and storing ammunition and the

## I WAS THERE

*We were not fired at previous to turning, possibly because they could not make us out as friend or enemy, but they then rectified the error and got our range quickly. Having fired torpedoes, we proceeded east at full speed to join our own fleet. We were in sight of the German battleships for ten minutes and were hit five times. High speed and zigzagging saved us from annihilation.*

Commodore C.E. Le Mesurier, Royal Navy[20]

training of gun crews. Now, crew members were completely interchangeable in the event of wounds or sickness. These new guns could also boast an impressive rate of fire – a rate of two rounds per minute was usual – which negated one of the key advantages smaller-calibre guns had previously held over larger naval weapons. Having guns of the same calibre also made it easier to calculate the trajectory and range of guns based on the splashes they made in the sea. If there were guns of different sizes firing at the same time, this could be a confusing task.

Although HMS *Dreadnought* carried ten big guns, the numbers differed in other similar classes of ship, and these were not the only armament carried. Smaller, lighter guns were carried to defend against torpedo boats and submarines, and some Dreadnoughts also had torpedoes. HMS *Dreadnought* carried twenty-two 12-pounder guns, and each could achieve a rate of fire of fifteen rounds per minute, which could make life very tough for any hostile small vessel. However, by 1914 the Royal Navy had increased the size of these secondary guns to 6in calibre.

With all the extra weight of these massive guns and the bigger shells it was important that HMS *Dreadnought* didn't compromise on speed. In fact, with the addition of brand-new

**DID YOU KNOW?**

HMS *Dreadnought* did not take part in the Battle of Jutland, as she was being refitted at the time. Throughout the conflict HMS *Dreadnought* sank one enemy U-boat – U-29 – in 1915.

steam turbines, HMS *Dreadnought* was actually quicker than most pre-Dreadnoughts, with a top speed of 22 knots and had a longer range.

Not surprisingly, the appearance of HMS *Dreadnought* sent navies throughout the world into mild panic. Germany especially became obsessed with meeting the Royal Navy head-on, and over the next few years a naval arms race ensued. The Royal Navy launched twenty-three more Dreadnought-class battleships up until 1914 and launched another eleven during the war itself, whilst Germany completed seventeen before the outbreak of war and another two before the armistice. Other major naval powers got in on the act too, including France, Italy and the USA.

After all of this chest-beating, the First World War itself was rather underwhelming from a

Dreadnought point of view. There was only one naval clash of note in which significant Dreadnought action took place – the Battle of Jutland in 1916 – and that particular battle was in itself nothing but indecisive. Germany ended the war with its entire fleet of Dreadnoughts intact and the Royal Navy only lost two: HMS *Audacious* sank after hitting a mine in October 1914 and HMS *Vanguard* sank due to an internal explosion in 1917.

# GERMAN U-BOATS

LIKE MANY OF the weapons used in the First World War, submerged marine warfare was only in its infancy when war broke out in 1914. The first German submarines (or U-boats) were completed in 1906, with long-range diesel-powered boats in service by 1913. It was true that at the outbreak of war the German Navy possessed the most advanced submarine service in the world, but even it only had ten working machines capable of operating against warships, with another eighteen older boats being used for training and coastal defence.

There were, however, some spectacular early successes, most notably the sinking of HMS *Aboukir*, *Cressy* and *Hogue* by U-9 on 22 September 1914 and the sinking of the battleship HMS *Formidable* on New Year's Day 1915.

Despite these early wins, many of the traditional German naval officers were very sceptical of the value of the U-boats. The early boats were too slow to spring a surprise on enemy ships, many had no surface guns and their slow dive times made them very vulnerable once they were spotted. Despite these issues, they quickly proved their worth, accounting for 396 out of the 468 Allied or neutral ships lost in 1915.

A big factor in the high percentage of hits for submarines at that time was the 'unrestricted submarine warfare' that Germany waged for

**DID YOU KNOW?**

The term U-boat is derived from the German *Unterseeboot* (literally 'undersea boat') and was used by all Allied countries to describe all German submarines, although the U prefix was only officially used for the larger, long-range craft, not for the smaller UB and UC classes.

seven months of the year in the hope it would bring Britain to its knees. This 'sink on sight' strategy was favoured by the admirals and senior naval staff, but the politicians of the time were less keen to keep such a strategy going for fear of bringing the USA into the war on the side of the Allies. In 1916 a compromise was agreed upon; enemy ships inside the 'war zone' that encircled the British Isles would be sunk without warning and if they were spotted outside this 'war zone' they would be attacked in a similar vein if they were armed. Passenger ships would not be harmed, regardless of where they were.

However, only a matter of weeks after this was announced to the world, U-29 sank the British passenger steamer *Sussex*. Three US

## I WAS THERE

We had perhaps been going for an hour and a half, keeping as close to the rocky coast as was safe, when above the roar of the storm there sounded a deeper, more reverberating roar – the roar of an explosion. Soon afterwards the Hampshire listed alarmingly to starboard and began to sink.

*Stoker Walter Charles Farnden, Royal Navy, one of only twelve survivors from the sinking of HMS Hampshire by a mine laid by a German U-boat[21]*

**DID YOU KNOW?**

The most successful U-boat in the First World War was U-35, which was responsible for sinking 538,498 tonnes of Allied shipping (226 separate ships) until it was formally handed over on 26 November as part of the German surrender.

citizens were among the dead and not surprisingly the USA acted angrily, demanding that Germany end its current method of submarine warfare. The threats fell on deaf ears and the hits kept coming. On 5 June the British armoured cruiser HMS *Hampshire* struck a mine laid by submarines off the Orkneys, sinking within minutes, with the loss of 643 lives, including Lord Kitchener, the British Minister of War.

In total, Germany manufactured and launched 375 U-boats during the war. These ships can be organised into seven distinct types: boats for export, gasoline-powered boats, ocean-going diesel-powered attack boats, cruisers and merchant U-boats, UB coastal torpedo attack boats, UC coastal minelayers and UE ocean minelayers.

The requirements for submarine warfare largely dictated design. Increased range, faster surface speeds and better torpedoes were the obvious improvements that were always needed, but as tactics developed, more specific design changes were requested from the crews. Better guns that could disable small ships whilst saving torpedoes was one such request, which saw surface guns grow steadily up to 150mm.

The UC-boats were designed specifically for laying mines. Introduced in the summer of 1915 they were able to lay small minefields that were very difficult to spot, making them a very useful weapon, sinking more than a million tonnes of Allied shipping during the course of the war. By 1916 a second version of the UC-boat was ready. Bigger and faster, it could cruise for more than 11,000km and could carry eighteen mines in addition to its three torpedo tubes and 88mm gun for surface attacks. A third class of UB-boat was commissioned in 1917 but never saw active service.

U-boats were especially effective against merchant and commercial shipping, and in 1917 they came close to achieving decisive results, sinking 2,439 ships in that year alone. However, there were simply not enough U-boats patrolling the seas at any given time to really cause a major problem to the Allies. Wartime losses were high, with 192 boats lost before the armistice and over 5,400 men killed.

# ALLIED SUBMARINES

ALTHOUGH THE GERMAN U-boat fleet dominated submarine warfare during the First World War, the Allied navies also made use of submarines too and achieved significant, if not spectacular, success.

All of the main Allied nations had some form of submarine force active during the war. Indeed, in 1914 France had the largest pre-war fleet in the world consisting of more than 120 boats, although in reality many of them were not capable of useful wartime service. Despite being obvious pioneers in this field, France and Britain entered into an agreement that French submarines would largely operate in the Mediterranean and not the North Sea or Atlantic, and as such they had only a limited opportunity to show the world what they could do. In addition, Italy boasted twenty-five boats and Russia had about forty, although most of these were purchased from other countries and were old and outdated.

Britain started the war with considerably more submarines than Germany. However, whereas Germany had concentrated its pre-war design and construction on longer-range offensive types of boat, the British had many more small vessels designed for coastal defence, with only a handful of diesel-powered 'D' Class submarines that were capable of taking the fight to the enemy.

# I WAS THERE

We were on patrol and the skipper said to me 'Tracy, what's that up there?' This was about half past three or four o'clock in the morning, it was just getting light. I said 'It's a silver cloud sir'. He said 'I wish to God it was, that's a blasted Zeppelin.' So down we go. Next thing I know we were down to 90ft. She dropped a bomb, nearly killed us all. We shot down to the bottom or nearly the bottom, about 90ft and there we laid [sic] and waited. Well I think we had another 6 or 7 explosions.

Seaman Owen Reynold Tracy, K-12 Submarine, 12th Submarine Flotilla, Royal Navy[22]

The successor to the 'D' Class was the 'E' Class, and in the early stages of the war these new boats enjoyed some success. E-9, under the command of Max Horton, was particularly successful, accounting for the sinking of the German light cruiser *Hela* and the German destroyer S-116 in the North Sea in mid-September. Shortly afterwards the majority of the German fleet was moved out to the Baltic and a fleet of British 'E' Class boats quickly followed them to bolster the Russian fleet, which was struggling with a shortage of (German-built) engines for their submarines. The main objective in the Baltic wasn't to go after the German fleet, although a couple of military vessels were attacked, but instead to disrupt the merchant shipping lanes that were sending critical supplies to German from Sweden.

The 'E' boats were well armed with five torpedo tubes and a decent 12-pounder deck gun. They also had decent surface speed, but were mechanically less reliable than their German counterparts and had limited wireless communications systems. On long journeys many submarine commanders had to rely on carrier pigeon for communications.

'E' boats were also used in the Dardanelles campaign, practically destroying the Turkish

**DID YOU KNOW?**

One of the reasons Allied submarines were not as successful as German U-boats was that the blockaded Central Powers simply didn't have enough merchant ships to be hunted.

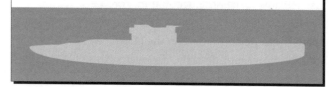

merchant shipping fleet as it crossed the Sea of Marmara. By the time Allied ground troops had been pulled out of the Gallipoli peninsula, the submarines represented the only ray of light in what was an otherwise disastrous Allied campaign. British and French submarines had accounted for two Turkish battleships, one destroyer, five gunboats, seven supply ships, nine troop transport vessels and over 220 other ships of various size and stature.

The 'E' type was regularly improved on during the war and became the mainstay of the British fleet. Eighty-eight 'E' type boats were built in total from 1914–18, including a number of minelayers and a few experimental versions, including the huge 'K' type submarine, which never got to see action.

With 137 serving boats and another seventy-eight being constructed, the Royal Navy had the largest Allied fleet at the end of the war, although it did suffer fifty-four losses, including seven boats scuttled in the Baltic after the signing of the Treaty of Brest-Litovsk.

# NOTES

1 MacDonald, Lyn, *1915: The Death of Innocence* (Penguin, 1993).

2 *The War Stories of Thomas Atkins* (London, 1914) p. 76.

3 MacDonald, Lyn, *Somme* (Penguin, 1993).

4 Middlebrook, Martin, *The First Day on the Somme* (Penguin, 1984).

5 Ibid.

6 Hammerton, John (ed.), *The Great War ... I Was There!* (The Amalgamated Press Ltd, 1939) p. 1481.

7 MacDonald, Lyn, *Somme* (Penguin, 1993).

8 Duffy, Francis P., *Father Duffy's Story* (George H. Doran Company, 1919).

9 MacDonald, Lyn, *1915: The Death of Innocence* (Penguin 1993).

10 Ibid. p. 439.

11 Hammerton, John (ed.), *The Great War ... I Was There!* (The Amalgamated Press Ltd, 1939) p. 1,783.

12 MacDonald, Lyn, *1915: The Death of Innocence* (Penguin 1993).

13 Morton, Desmond, *When Your Number's Up: The Canadian Soldier in the First World War* (Random House of Canada, 1993).

14 Hammerton, John (ed.), *The Great War ... I Was There!* (The Amalgamated Press Ltd, 1939) p. 1,831.

15 Purdom, C.B. (ed.), *Everyman at War* (1930).

16  Arthur, Max, *Forgotten Voices of the Great War* (Ebury Press, 2003).

17  Hammerton, John (ed.), *The Great War ... I Was There!* (The Amalgamated Press Ltd, 1939) p. 453.

18  Whitehouse, A.G. J., *Hell in the Heavens* (W. & R. Chambers, 1938).

19  Hammerton, John (ed.), *The Great War ... I Was There!* (The Amalgamated Press Ltd, 1939) p. 319.

20  Bennett, Geoffrey, *Naval Battles of the First World War* (Penguin, 1968).

21  Farnden, Walter C., 'Alive to Tell the Tale', in *The Sydney Morning Herald*, Saturday 19 November 1938.

22  IWM Cat. No. 24529.

Discover more books in this series ...

5 MINUTE HISTORY

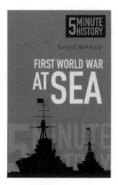

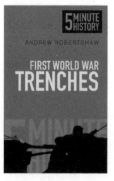
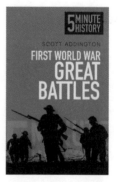
Visit our website and discover thousands
of other History Press books.

**www.thehistorypress.co.uk**

The History Press